TREE-HOUSE COMIX PROUDLY PRESENTS

DOG MAN
A TALE OF TWO KITTIES

WRITTEN AND ILLUSTRATED BY **DAV PILKEY**

AS GEORGE BEARD AND HAROLD HUTCHINS

WITH COLOR BY JOSE GARIBALDI

graphix

AN IMPRINT OF

SCHOLASTIC

HERE'S TO YOU, MR. ROBINSON!
(THANK YOU, DICK.)

Scholastic Children's Books
An imprint of Scholastic Ltd
Euston House, 24 Eversholt Street, London, NW1 1DB, UK
Registered office: Westfield Road, Southam, Warwickshire, CV47 0RA
SCHOLASTIC and associated logos are trademarks and/or
registered trademarks of Scholastic Inc.

First published in the US by Scholastic Ltd, 2017
First published in the UK by Scholastic Ltd, 2018

Copyright © Dav Pilkey, 2017

The right of Dav Pilkey to be identified as the
author and illustrator of this work has been asserted by him.

ISBN 978 1407 18667 2
A CIP catalogue record for this book
is available from the British Library.

Printed in China
Papers used by Scholastic Children's Books are made
from wood grown in sustainable forests.

5 7 9 10 8 6

This is a work of fiction. Names, characters, places, incidents
and dialogues are products of the author's imagination or are used
fictitiously. Any resemblance to actual people, living or dead,
events or locales is entirely coincidental.

www.scholastic.co.uk

Chapters

DOG MAN

Behind the scenes

Hi, everybody. It's your old pals, George and Harold.

Yo, what up, dogs?

We're in 5th grade now. We're older and wiser...

... and Totally mature, I might add.

We even got a new teacher named Ms. Chivess. She's Pretty cool...

... except for one thing. She makes us read classic Literature.

Moby-Dick

This month we're reading <u>A Tale of Two Cities</u>.

And we're having a dickens of a time!!!

HA HA HA HA HA HA HA HA HA HA

Like we said, we're totally mature now.

Anyway, we didn't think we'd like it, but it's actually pretty good.

A Tale of Two Cities
Charles Dickens

Yeah. It's <u>deep</u> and stuff.

It inspired us to make a brand new DOG MAN graphic novel!

Now we're DEEP, Too!

DOG MAN
a Tale of Two Kitties

And So... Tree House comix ProudLy Presents:

A Tale of oppression...

chief

...a Tale of redemption...

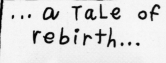

... a Tale of rebirth...

... and a tale of hope.

A TALE OF TWO KiTTieS

But First...

... a recap of our story thus far:

DOG MAN

supa Recap!

They were the best of cops...

They were the worst of cops.

...it was an epoch of inspiration.

I Know! Let's sew the dog's head onto the cop's body!!!!

Hooray!

Yay!

It was a procedure of Precariousness...

...it was a surgery of Success.

HOORAY FOR DOG MAN!

There was a cop with a dog's head on the cold streets of a savage city...

...There was a cat with a wicked heart enchained in Kitty Custody.

Rats!

Cat Jail

And so begins our Tale of mirth and woe.

It ain't easy being deep and mature...

... but somebody's gotta do it!

Tree-
House
comix
proudly
presents

DOGMAN

Chapter the First:
Recalled to Duty

chief

By GEORge and Harold

15

How MANy Times hAve we TALKED About This?

That's **No Way** For a cop To behave!

I'm gettin' **TiReD** of This !!

Tired, Tired, **TiRED!**

Hey, ChieF. Didn't you want to Show Dog MAn the news?

Oh, Yeah!

LOOK! WE'RE HEROES...

...because we saved the world from FLIPPY!!!

Lick
Lick
Lick

It says here that scientists ~~too~~ are going to study FLIPPY's brain!

DOG MAN, I have an important job for you!

I'm putting you in charge of security!

Who wants to protect the scientists?

Well, Flippy is a dead fish.

Remember how Dog Man likes to roll around in dead fish?

Aw, he'd never do anything like that!

Dog Man is a Good Doggy!

KLUNK

meanwhile...

CAT JAIL

OH, boy! OH, boy!

Today is my birthday, and the warden gave me all of these balloons!!!

Here's one for you, Tippy!

and here's one for you, Fluffy!

27

Home at Last!

Petey's Secret Lab

28

STEP 1: insert DNA into DNA Chute.

TWING

DNA CHUTE

START

STEP 2: Press Start Button.

Directions

DNA

CHUNKA CHUNKA CHUNKA

Ding!

Step 3: Open door to retrieve your clone.

33

HeLLo, I'm Dr. Dookie from "The Supa Awesome science center over There".

Our team of Science dudes just returned from the mountain.

we went there To dig up Flippy the Psychokinetic Fish.

Why'd ya dig him up?

'Cuz we wanna Study his amazing brain. D_uh_!

But I thought Flippy was dead!!!

He is!

But fortunately, he was perfectly preserved in ice.

Show 'em, DOG Man!

See? Not a scratch on him!

What wonders can Flippy's brain teach us?

STEP 1.
First, place your left hand inside the dotted lines marked "left hand here". Hold the book open FL<u>A</u>T!

STEP 2:
Grasp the right-hand page with your thumb and index finger (inside the dotted lines marked "Right Thumb Here").

STEP 3:
Now QUICKL<u>Y</u> flip the right-hand page back and forth until the picture appears to be A<u>nimated</u>.

(for extra fun, try adding your own sound-effects!)

O.RAMA

Remember,

while you are flipping,
be sure you can see
the image on page **43**
AND the image on page **45.**

If you flip quickly,
the two pictures will
start to look like
one **ANimated** cartoon!

Don't forget to
add your own
sound-effects!

Left
hand here.

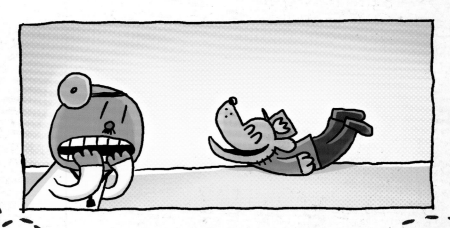

Right
Thumb
here.

Aw, why do you guys gotta be so mean to DOG Man?

He broke every bone in this fish's body!!!!

So what? It was already dead!!!!

HOW Are we supposed To STudy The brain of a Squished fish???

I Know! We can rebuild him!!!

we can make him better than he was!

Faster---
Stronger---
Fishier!!!

That's a Good idea! Let's Go back to the "Supa Awesome Science Center Over there"!!!

Ok!

Come on, Dog Man! You can help us!!!

But you still have to Look sad!

That's better!!!

The Supa Awesome Science Center Over There

Soon, the scientists had a big operation.

They replaced all of Flippy's broken bones...

...with bionics!

Flippy was now more machine than fish.

Boy, it's a good thing Flippy is dead!

I know! He'd be _so_ Dangerous if he ever came back to Life!!!

Yeah--- with his telekinetic brain AND bionic super strength? He'd be **unSTOPPable**!!!

Well, I'm glad we don't have to worry about that!

Me too! With Dog Man guarding him, what could go wrong?

Let's go home and get some rest!

Good idea!

51

Oh, Hi DOG Man!

How did your security Job go?

Why are you hiding behind that plant?

Were you a bad doggy?

Did you do a bad thing?

What did you do?

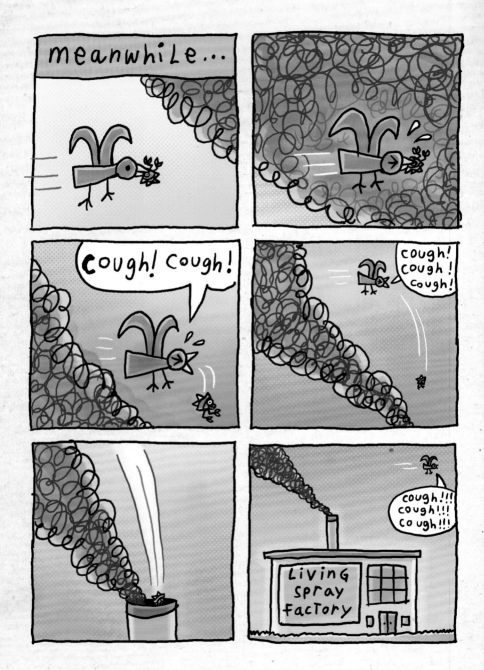

Chapter The fourth
No More Kitten AROUND!

Free kitty

60

Later...

Hey Papa!

Look! I made you a book!

Why don't you go make me a cup of tea instead?

OK

Soon...

It's about time!!!

JUST GET IN!

but why?

we're gonna play a game!

It's called the "New Home" game.

FREE KITTY

This is just for Pretend though, right?

of course!

And so...

Free KITTY

66

He doesn't have a name!

I do too have a name! My name's "Li'L Petey."

Heh-heh. Don't listen to him.

You can call him whatever you want!

I think I'll call you "Snowball"!!!

I think I'll call you "Poo-Poo head."

HOW RUDE!

Bye-Bye, Poo-Poo head!

Free Kitty

Alright, wise Guy, Next Time Let **ME** do the Talking!

Free KITTY

I don't wanna be here all day!

I gotta go Potty.

Free

Just hold it, Man!

Free

Gee **Whiz!** What is **WRONG** with everybody these days?

It makes ya worry about the future!

"Duh, how much does he cost?"

WHAT AN IDIOT!!

I mean, The sign **CLEARLY** says...

Life is hard and filled with fright...

...for my little crate and me...

...We are all alone tonight...

...filled with sad uncertainty...

74

Chapter the Fifth
CRATE EXPECTATIONS

Li'L PeTeY!

CoMe OUT, CoMe OUT, WhereVer YoU Are !!!!

TWO hours Later...

Perey's Secret Lab

Papa and me
by Lil Petey

Papa and me go to our car

Look at Papa's new invention

Papa and me think the same things.

SMOKESTACK FILTER

Hey, what's this?!!?

I'm not sure. It looks like some sort of evil, bionic, psychokinetic, dead fish!

But how did it get stuck in our smoke-stack?

And who could be responsible for such a thing?

Meanwhile 3.0

ZZZZ

chief

HeY!!!

chief

what are you doing behind that plant?

chief

No, wait---

chief

NOOOOO

BAD DOGGY!!

I WAS ONLY GONE FOR TEN Seconds!

DoG Man, there's a cat outside.

You need to get rid of him!

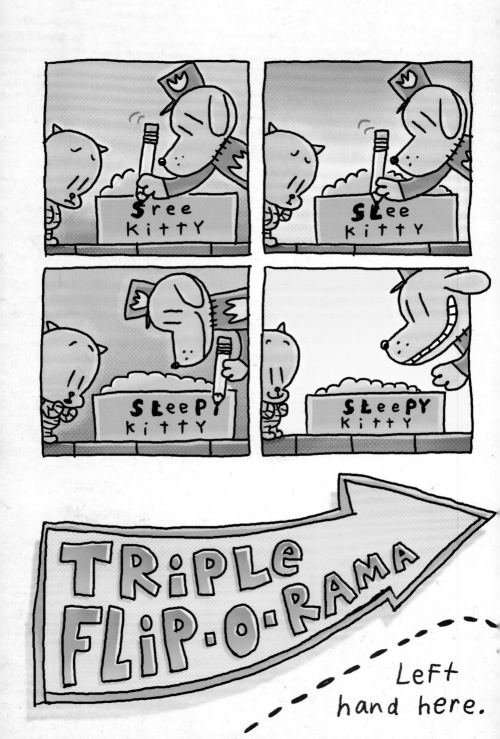

BRUSH
BRUSH
BRUSH

Jump
Jump
Jump

Kiss
Kiss
Kiss

Right Thumb here.

Brush
Brush
Brush

Jump
Jump
Jump

Kiss
Kiss
Kiss

CHAPTER THE SIXTH

Tree-House Comix Proudly Presents

A BUNCHA STUFF THAT HAPPENED NEXT!

FLIP FLOP FLIP FLOP FLIP

BY GEORGE AND HAROLD

Meanwhile...

PeTeY'S
Secret
Lab

CLOP!

At Last! MY 80-Hexotron Droid-formigon is complete!!!

OK, bub. I need you To Scan this comic.

chunka Chunka Chunka

Now Go find the kid who made it!

And So...

FLiP FLop FLiP FLop FLiP FLop

FLiP FLoP FLiP FLoP FLiP

Flip Flop Flip

Flip Flop Flip

WeLL, weLL, weLL!!!! I Should have Known!

DOG Man

Don't just stand there! **Get Him!!!**

DOG man

And so...

Oh, hi Papa.

Don't call me Papa!!!

Hey, where's Dog Man?

Dog Man isn't here.

Dog Man is my friend!

Dog Man saved me from ~~the~~ a buncha weirdos.

DOG Man Goes "Grrrrrr!"

RUFF! RUFF! RUFF!

RUFF RUFF RUFF RUFF!

WOULd You CUT That out?!!?

RUFF! RUFF! RUFF!

TWO HOURS LATER...

...And then these weird guys wanted to dye my fur pink, so DOG Man goes "**Grrrr!**"

then DoG Man goes, "**Ruff Ruff Ruff Ruff!**

And Dog Man scared 'em away! And Then...

ENOUGH ABOUT DOG MAN!

RUFF RUFF

RUFF!

Hey, Look! It's DOG Man!!!!

Watch and Learn, Kid!!!

Petey, the world's most smartest cat, proudly presents:

The **TRUE** story of Dog Man!

La La La ... Duh, Hi! I'm Dog Man!

I'm a big dummy!

I like to chase cars and drink out of the toilet !!!

HA HA HA HA HA HA HA HA HA

119

OH! Look who's here! It's Petey!!!

Look at me! I'm sooo smart! I'm totally cool!

I build Awesome robots and other cool stuff!!!!

I'm gonna rule the world one day!

Hey, do Dog Man again!

NO! DOG MAN is DUMB!!!

PeTeY iS A GENiUS!!!

He's so cool and awesome and handsome!!!!

Everybody wants to be like Petey!

Meanwhile...

DOG Man

SLEEPY KITTY

Z Z Z Z

SLEEPY KITTY

Ring
Ring

SWOOSH!

Hi, Dog Man!

It's me, Sarah. How's it going?

RUFF!

OH, NO! We'LL be right over!!!!!

What's the problem, Dog Man?

LoST KiTTY
if FounD CALL COPS!

Come on! Let's make some copies and spread 'em around!!!!!

Well, what should we do with this dead fish thingy?

Let's get rid of it!

We don't want it stinkin' up the place!!!

O.K.

Trash

Meanwhile...

PeTeY's
Secret
LaB

Rise and
shine,
Kid!!

Gimme that!

swipe

HEY!

Just forget about
Dog Man for a
minute!

We've got important
Stuff to do Today!

Can he play duck-duck-goose?

Yeah, but--- **NO!!!** Why would you want to---

Listen, kid: **YOU'RE MY CLONE!!!**

That means **YOU** are the **SAME** as **Me!**

Your soul is wretched just like mine!

You've got a whole lifetime of evilness ahead of you!

Look, kid, I just programmed 80-HD to obey your every command!!!

Once you feel the **POWER** in your **PAWS**...

...I'm sure that your evil side will rise to the surface.

Go ahead--- Make him **DO SOMETHING!**

Seriously! He'll do **Anything** you want!!!

Anything?

TRiPLE FLiP-O-RAMA

Left hand here.

Right
Thumb
here.

But supa Mecha Flippy was not the **ONLY** thing coming to Life.

As the Living spray gas spread throughout the Factory...

...the Factory began coming to Life, Too!

GOOBA GABA!

Living Spray Factory

This **BEASTY BUILDING** is just what I need to help me get **REVENGE!!!**

141

Soon, the Living Spray Factory ran out of gas...

Uh-oh.

...but not before it had created a whole army of **Beasty Buildings!**

Haw Haw Haw!!! And I'm controlling them all with my supa mind powers!!!

Meanwhile...

Petey's Secret Lab

HeY!!!!

That Robot is **NOT** your "**FRIEND**"!

This is **SERIOUS**!!! It's **NOT PLAYTIME**!

Open up, 80-HD!

I said, **OPEN UP, 80-HD!**

Oh, yeah. I forgot. I just programmed 80-HD to obey **YOUR** commands.

Tell him to open up.

Open up, 80-HD!

SHOOOP!

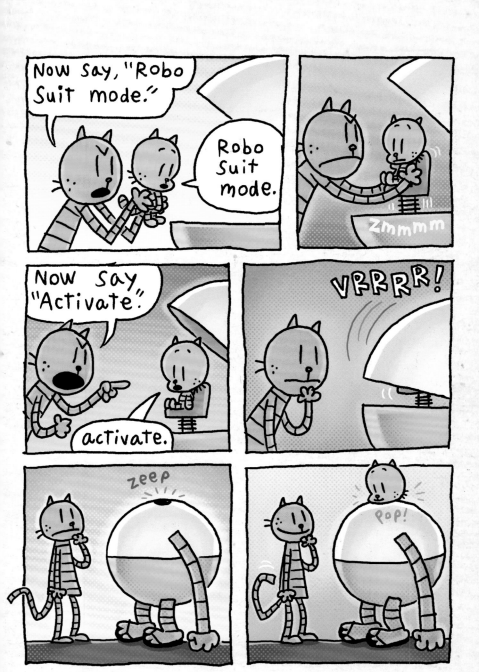

Left hand here.

Petting Papa

Disco Papa

Rock -a- Bye Papa

Right Thumb here.

Petting
Papa

Disco
Papa

Rock
-a-
Bye
Papa

YOU'RE DRIVING ME CRAY-CRAY!

PETEY's SECRET LAB

But then...

wee-ooo-wee-ooo-wee

chief

Screech!

LOST KITTY
IF FOUND CALL COP

LOST KITTY
IF FOUND CALL COP

chief

Hey Gang! A buncha buildings came to Life, and they're about to attack!

chief

Los KIT IF call

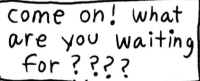

Quick, Chief. Grab the end of this dental floss...

... and tie it around that sign across the street.

TRIP

CRASH

FrencH
saLad
Dressing

Slippery
when
wet

DOG Man and ZuZu
watched the action...

CH
AD
NG

Slippery
when
wet

CH
AD
NG

...then they got an
idea of their own!

VRMMM

EMERGENCY
Brake

FRENCH
SALAD
DRESSING

ReLease
BUTTON

ReLease
BUTTON

CLICK

And then...

Hey, what's all that noise?

Let's find out!

FLiP FLoP FLiP FLoP

CRASH!

Petey's Secret Lab

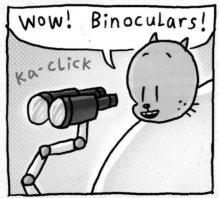

Chapter the Eighth

THE French DRESSING REVOLUTION

French SALAD Dressing

HEY! What happened over Here?

MY BEAUTIFUL BEASTY Buildings!

WHO COULD HAVE DONE SUCH a THING???

Hey ChieF, Let's help Dog Man and ZUZU destroy Some more buildings!

OK!

chief

It looked
like this
was the
end...

Oh well, at least Dog Man and Zuzu are safe!

They're **not** safe!!! They're **FALLING**!!!

Who will save them?

He takes a Lickin'
and keeps on Tickin'!!!

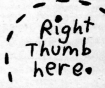

Right
Thumb
here.

He takes a Lickin'
and Keeps on Tickin' !!!

Left hand here.

Right
Thumb
here.

And so...

WHUMP

HOORAY!!!

Those jerks may have defeated my Beasty Buildings...

...but they're no match for my psychokinetic mind powers!!!

I think I'll start by getting rid of this Robo-cat!

189

Li'L Petey! Are you okay?

Yeah. But 80-HD Got broke!!!

Don't worry. He can be repaired.

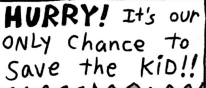

195

Ready or Not...

...Here I come!

Meanwhile, it looked like the gang had escaped.

Hey, it's my cop car!

Let's hide out in this building.

Ok!

ART SUPPLIES

Hurry!

And soon...

ART SUPPLI

Meanwhile...

Hmmm... How should I get rid of this guy?

I know! I'll drop him into that volcano over there!!!

And once he is gone...

...I'll destroy Dog Man and his "heroic" friends!!!

Hi, Dog Man!

ROOF ROOF ROOF!

Oh, yes. I see you've noticed our **ROOF!** We have a new sign!

PLease feeL free to test drive any of our fine Products!

Meanwhile...

...Things were not Looking very good for Petey. He was being Lifted higher and higher by the mighty brain powers of Supa Mecha Flippy.

HAW HAW HAW!

As soon as he reaches 10,000 feet, I'LL drop him into that volcano!

But then...

SCREECH

HEY! WATCH where you're driving, Lead-Foot!!!

Hi, FLippy. What'cha doing?

the End!

I'm very busy destroying This Robo-cat!

why?

'cuz he's a **Jerk!**

why?

Because, uh...

...because nobody likes me.

Why?

I don't know.

Nobody has ever liked me. Even back in school...

...the other fish never played with me.

They called me "Fatty Fish Lips"!

I'm sorry.

Hey, I know what will cheer you up!

Look! I made you a book!

my Friend FLiPPY

Do ya wanna read it?

OK.

my Fr

And so...

The End.

my Friend FLiPPY

FLIPPY
and me
FLEW UP
TO a star.

they had
a swing set
so we
swinged
on it.

I FELL
OFF BUT
FLIPPY
saved me.

FLippy and me went under the sea

then we ate Five soups.

The End.

Did'ja like it?

It was... it was...

Beautiful!!!

AS Flippy's evil heart melted, something strange began to happen...

OH, NO!!! My---My evil Powers!!!

They're--- they're getting WEAKER!

Uh-oh!

This was not good news for Petey.

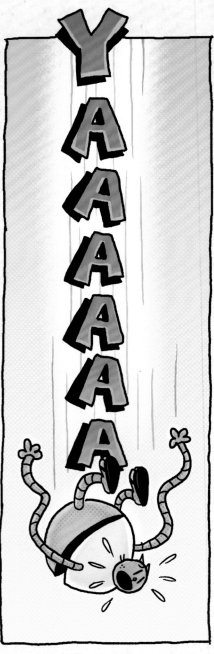

Oh well...

...I guess this is the end.

GOOD-BYE, CRUEL world!

It is a far, far better...

...Rest that I go to...

...than I have ever known!

WOW!
Thanks, Dog Man!!!

cLick

RATS!!!

Tree-
House
Comix
Proudly
Presents

Chapter the Tenth

THREE Endings

by George and Harold

The FiRST ENDiNG
FLiPPY'S STORY

Soon, everyone was safely on the ground.

HOORAY FOR DOGMAN!

chief

Phooey!

But then...

FLippy, you've been a naughty fish Today!

I know.

ZUZU and I are making a citizen's arrest!

OK.

But before I go...

Could I borrow this book for a while?

You can keep it! I made it for you!

really?

Yeah! I'll make **more** if ya want!

OK.

Let's be pen pals! We can make books for each other!

Ok!

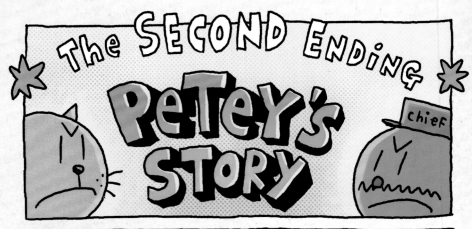

The SECOND ENDiNG
PETEY'S STORY

Meanwhile, back in the Present...

ALRight, Petey! I'm taking you to JaiL!

Why? What'd I do???

You escaped on page 27, remember?

Oh, yeah.

WeLL, Kid, it Looks Like you'LL be staying with Dog Man for a while.

Ok.

You know, Chief, I've gotta change my ways!!!

Yep.

Cat Jail

I mean, I've got a kid now!

I know!

I can't be goin' around being a jerk all the Time!

That's Right!

I've gotta be **RESPONSIBLE!!!**

I Agree!

I've gotta be a **ROLE MODEL!!!**

So true!

I've gotta be **GOOD!!!**

ABSOLUTELY!!!

225

The Third Ending
Li'l Petey's Story

Hey Look! Here's his other Flip-Flop!

It took forever, but we finally got all of the pieces!

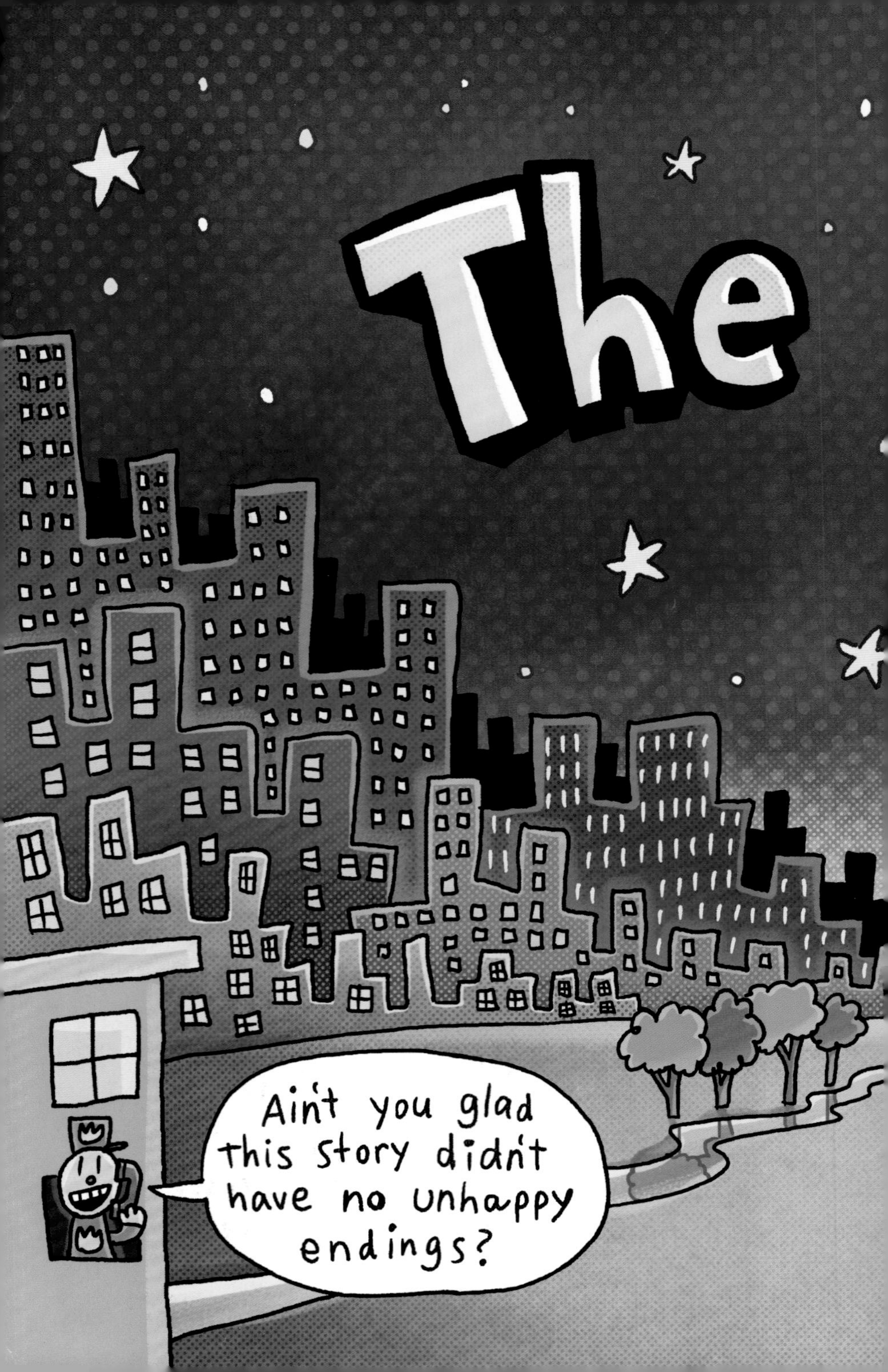
The
Ain't you glad this story didn't have no unhappy endings?

...if you thought our adventure was over...

YOU AiN'T READ NOTHiN' YET!

AT this very moment, George and Harold are busy creating their **NEXT** work of depth and maturity.

Take a peep, my peeps!

When a glamorous movie starlet disappears...

NEWS
YOLAY Caprese KidNapped

DOG Man is There to help!

RUFF RUFF RUFF
RUFF

RUFF
RUFF
RUFF
RUFF

But who will help Dog Man?

Find out in our next exciting EPiC NOVEL...

chief

235

...AND You Like Suspense...

...And you Like LAFFS...

...Then DOG MAN is GO!

DOG Man is GO? That don't make no sense!

BUT we Like it!

HOW 2 DRAW Li'L PeTeY

in 20 Ridiculously easy steps!

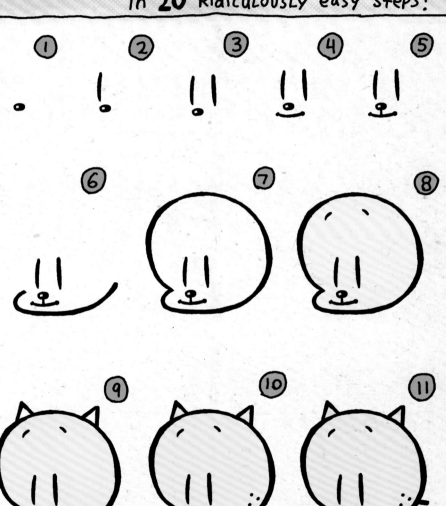

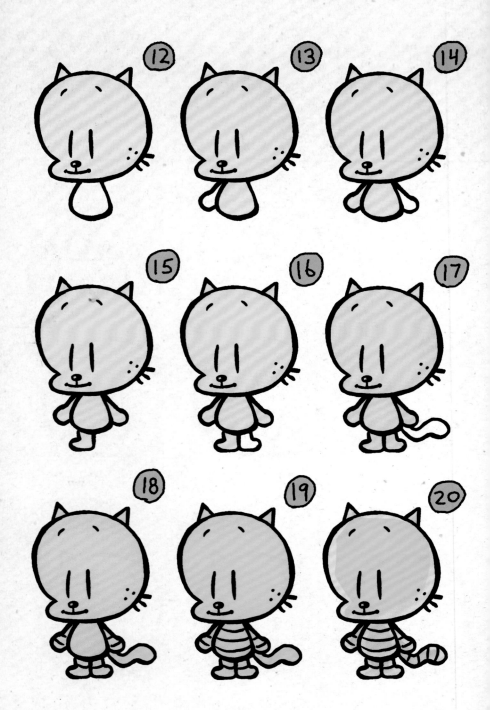

238

80-HD

in 18 Ridiculously easy Steps!

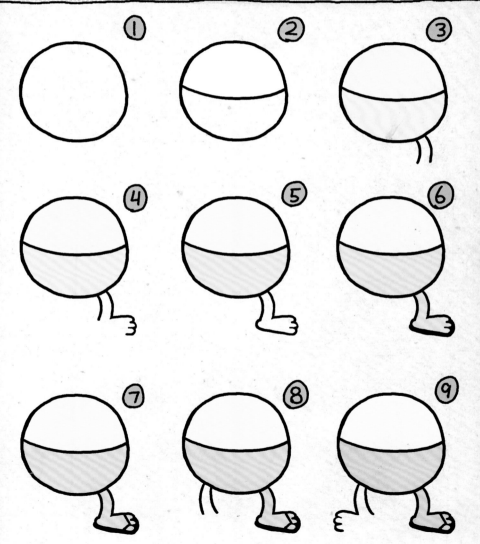

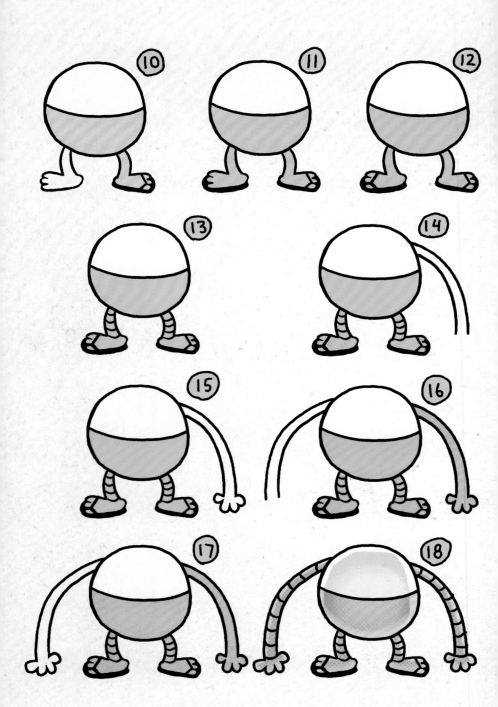

A BEASTY BUILDING

in **21** Ridiculously easy steps!

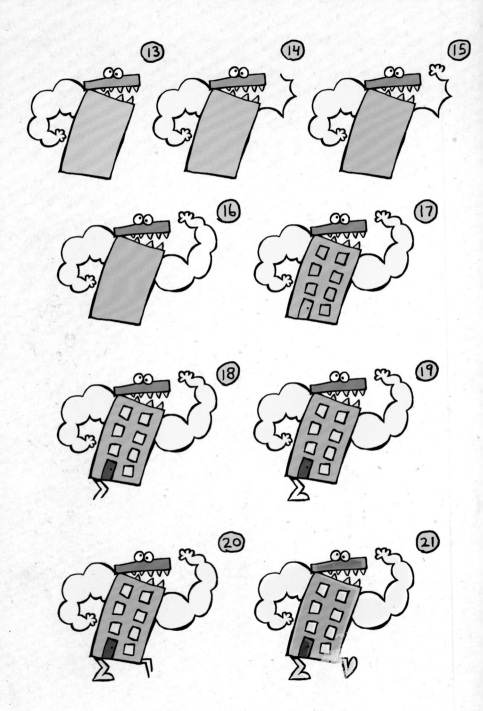

243

HOW 2 DRAW DOG MAN

in 34 Ridiculously easy Steps!

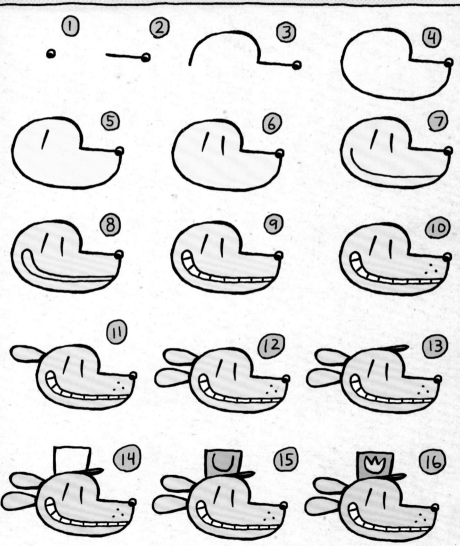

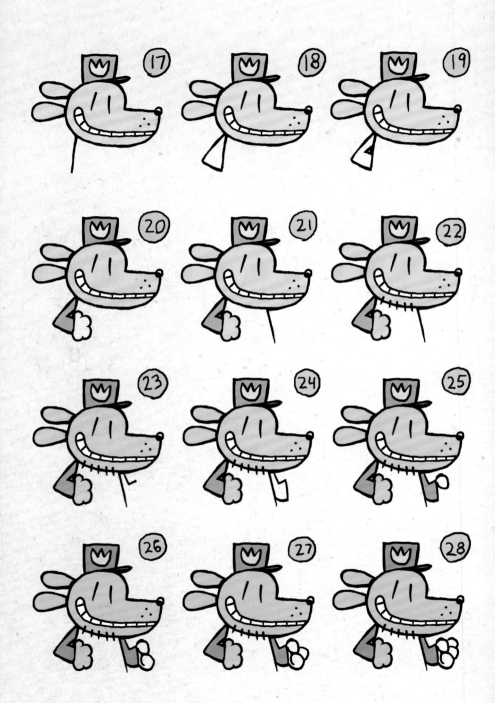

LEARN 2 DRAW MORE CHARACTERS at SCHOLASTIC.COM and PILKEY.COM

READ TO YOUR DOG, MAN!

But did you know there's a way to take your reading "skillz" to the **NEXT LEVEL?**

Just read to your dog, man!

Researchers have studied the benefits of reading out loud to dogs.

Here's what they discovered:

Kids who read out loud to dogs can improve their fluency by **12** to **30%**! *

I feel smarter already, man!

me too, man!

Plus, there are lots of other potential benefits, too:

* University of California-Davis: Reading to Rover, 2010

Reading to dogs has also been linked to increased empathy and kindness.

But what if ya don't have a dog, man?

DOGS →

Check with your local library or animal shelter!

They might have volunteer Dogs you can read to!

So take your reading to the next level, man...

... And read to your Dog, man!

READING TO YOUR DOG IS ALWAYS A PAWS-ITIVE EXPERIENCE!

SOPHIE, BRIDGET & JAC

MICHAEL, KADEN, WINSLOW, MILO, GAVIN & SOPHIA

BECKY & REESIE CUP

LUCAS & JACK

JOSH & REESIE CUP

REESIE CUP & AJ

LILY & SALMA

SERENITY & LILY

#ReadToYourDogMan

KATIE & REESIE CUP

GABRIEL, JACOB & GIZMO

KATE & BRIDGET

KRAMER & CAMERON

ADAM & REESIE CUP

CHEWIE, KYLE, TYGRA, ALEK & PEE WEE

LEARN MORE AT PILKEY.COM!

ABOUT THE AUTHOR-ILLUSTRATOR

When Dav Pilkey was a kid, he suffered from ADHD, dyslexia, and behavioral problems. Dav was so disruptive in class that his teachers made him sit out in the hall every day. Luckily, Dav loved to draw and make up stories. He spent his time in the hallway creating his own original comic books.

In the second grade, Dav Pilkey created a comic book about a superhero named Captain Underpants. His teacher ripped it up and told him he couldn't spend the rest of his life making silly books.

Fortunately, Dav was not a very good listener.

ABOUT THE COLORIST

Jose Garibaldi grew up on the South Side of Chicago. As a kid, he was a daydreamer and a doodler, and now it's his full-time job to do both. Jose is a professional illustrator, painter, and cartoonist who has created work for Dark Horse Comics, Disney, Nickelodeon, MAD Magazine, and many more. He lives in Los Angeles, California, with his wife and their cats.